It's my name and i'm the best Dad ever!

Happy Father's Day, Dad.

I smile because you're my father. I laugh because there's nothing you can do about it.

How do you get a squirrel to like you? Act like a nut.

Thanks for putting up with me, Dad!

Dad, you've always been the coolest – like all those times you said 'yes' when Mom said 'no.

What kind of shoes do ninjas wear? Sneakers!

This might sound cheesy, but you're the gratest, Dad.

Dad. He can play like a kid, give advice like a friend, and protect like a bodyguard.

Did you hear the rumor about butter? Well, I'm not going to spread it!

Not all heroes wear capes. Mine wears cargo shorts.

My father didn't tell me how to live.
He lived and let me watch him do it.

Why couldn't the bicycle stand up by itself? It was two tired

Worst jokes. Best dad.

Some people don't believe in heroes but they haven't met my dad

Dad, can you put the cat out?" "I didn't know it was on fire

You'll always be dad to the bone

A father is neither an anchor to hold us back nor a sail to take us there but a guiding light whose love shows us the way

What time did the man go to the dentist? Tooth hurt-y

Thanks for being the best role model I could ever imagine

You brought me every single toy that I wanted when I was young. I hope I can return the favor when I grow up by achieving every single goal that you always wanted me to. I love you

What concert costs just 45 cents? 50 Cent featuring Nickelback!

A dad is someone you look up to no matter how tall you grow

Nothing makes me feel stronger
than knowing that I have a dad
who's got my back. I love you

Why did the math book look so sad? Because of all of its problems!

My dad gives Superman a run for his money

You have seen me at my worst,
yet you think that I am the
best. I love you, Dad

How does a penguin build its house? Igloos it together

I know I don't say it enough, so
I'll say it extra today: Thank
you for everything, Dad

Dad, even a fleeting memory of your loving smile is enough to light up my darkest days. I love you!

I made a pencil with two erasers. It was pointless.

You're the best, Dad.
Plain and simple

Dad, you are my hero and my role model. Thanks for being here for me and being a great example

I'm reading a book about anti-gravity. It's impossible to put down!

Not always eye to eye, but always heart to heart

Dad: A son's first hero, a daughter's first love

Did you hear about the guy who invented the knock-knock joke? He won the 'no-bell' prize

life doesn't come with a manual
—it comes with a father

Dads are most ordinary men turned by love into heroes, adventurers, storytellers and singers of song

I've got a great joke about construction, but I'm still working on it

I love my dad to the moon and back

A dad is someone who wants to catch you when you fall. Instead he picks you up, brushes you off and lets you try again

I used to hate facial hair...but then it grew on me

Behind every great man/woman is an even better father

Dad, your guiding hand on my shoulder will remain with me forever

I had a neck brace fitted years ago and I've never looked back since

If I didn't have you as a dad, I'd want you as a friend

A father is neither an anchor to hold us back,
nor a sail to take us there, but a guiding light
whose love shows us the way

What's brown and sticky? A stick

Sorry everyone else, I have the best dad in the world

A truly rich man is one whose children run into his arms when his hands are empty

Why can't you hear a psychiatrist using the bathroom? Because the 'P is silent

Thanks for always being my anchor

The only thing better than having you for a husband is our children having you for a daddy

What do you call an elephant that doesn't matter? An irrelephant

You're so hip, you had a dad bod *before* it was cool

My Father's Day gift to you is letting you pretend to be in charge of the family for a day

What do you get from a pampered cow? Spoiled milk

I like telling Dad jokes. Sometimes he laughs!

In honor of Father's Day, I promise to laugh at all of your jokes

Did I tell you the time I fell in love during a backflip? I was heels over head!

We all know that Mom did the hard part. But Happy Father's Day anyway!

To the world you are a dad. To our family, you are the world

If a child refuses to sleep during nap time, are they guilty of resisting a rest?

Any man can be a Father it takes someone special to be a Dad

How do you make holy water?
You boil the hell out of it

The greatest gift I ever had came from God; I call him Dad!

I ordered a chicken and an egg online. I'll let you know.

____

____

____

____

____

____

____

____

____

____

____

To my father. If I can become
half the man he is, I'll have
achieved greatness

It takes guts to be an organ donor

If you see a crime at an Apple Store, does that make you an iWitness?

I'm so good at sleeping, I can do it with my eyes closed!

Two peanuts were walking down the
street. One was a salted

Here's to the man who is wisest and best. I mean the man who is "Dad" to me!

Can February March? No, but April May!

Did you hear about the circus fire? It was in tents.

The best thing having you as my Husband is our children having you as their daddy!

How do lawyers say goodbye?
We'll be suing ya!

Wanna hear a joke about paper?
Never mind—it's tearable.

Dad you are handy when you have to be, And pretty good at putting up with me

What's the best way to watch a fly fishing tournament? Live stream

Spring is here! I got so excited I wet my plants

I love how we all know I am your favorite child Dad!

I could tell a joke about pizza,
but it's a little cheesy

Don't trust atoms. They make up everything!

Here's to the man who with judgment is blessed

When does a joke become a dad joke? When it becomes apparent

I wouldn't buy anything with velcro. It's a total rip-off

What's an astronaut's favorite part of a computer? The space bar.

I don't play soccer because I enjoy the sport. I'm just doing it for kicks!

Why are elevator jokes so classic and good? They work on many levels

Why do bees have sticky hair? Because they use a honeycomb.

What do you call a fake noodle? An impasta

Which state has the most streets? Rhode Island

Here's to the man who's as smart as can be, I mean the man who is "Dad" to me!

What did the coffee report to the police? A mugging

I once had a dream I was floating in an ocean of orange soda. It was more of a fanta sea

I just watched a documentary about beavers. It was the best dam show I ever saw!

What is Beethoven's favorite fruit? A ba-na-na-na.

Where did the college-aged vampire like to shop? Forever 21.

9 798644 218233